Ed Kramer

ed@ejkramer.com

First edition Sept. 1, 2022

ISBN: 979-8-985723458

Welcome to San Miguel de Allende, Mexico

Book 1 in this Series

Where is My Mind?
The Adventure Has Begun
A Flippant View of Art, Science, Technology and Life
Available Now, Published 3/15/2022

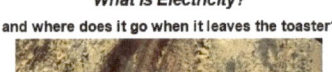

Book 2 in this Series

What is Electricity?
and where does it go when it leaves the toaster?
A brilliant experiment,,, On a cool dry day, scuff your feet along a carpet, then reach your hand into a friend's mouth and touch one of her dental fillings.
Available Now, Published 4/15/2022

DOORS & MORE...

The Magic of San Miguel de Allende, Mexico,,,

ED KRAMER

Margaret Henkel
Editor

This book is dedicated to my family who have
encouraged me both with my photography and with writing this book.

Professional Endorsements from Unpublished Authors:

This is a MUST READ for anyone thinking about travel to Mexico.

Rita Book, Librarian

Kramer's mind may be idea storage in a classical sense, but it seems to be clogged with a lot of irrelevant information.

Ho Lee Chit, Chinese Labor Bureau

Kramer undoubtedly wrote this book 'cause it was cheaper than golf.

Pat Agonia, Travel Agent

There is no shortage of Doors & Dolls in this publication,,,

Paige Turner, Wannabe Editor

Cozy up with a glass of tequila and turn on the music. This could become your favorite book.

Bertha D. Blues, Mariachi Band Leader

INTRODUCTION:

This book gives me a chance to share three of my passions, ARCHITECTURE, TRAVEL and PHOTOGRAPHY, with whimsical inserts of "Life Imitating Art" - or is it "Art Imitating Life?"

Life is like a CAMERA
Focus on the important
Capture the good times
Develop from the negative
And if things don't work out
TAKE ANOTHER SHOT,,,

When I am traveling, I always have my camera with me. The camera that I usually carry has always been one of those digital SLRs with a zoom lens. Yes, it is heavy and bulky, but it takes great photos.

Recently, I stepped into the modern age with one of those ''Smart Phones.'' You know, a pocket phone that has a camera built into it. (Boy, I wish I had thought of that combination!) Anyway, all of the photos in this book were taken with my new ''Smart Phone.'' I must say, the phone is a convenient package. Although it took a little getting used to, the photos came out great as you will see, but the digital SLR is still a lot more versatile device...

I used my camera as an all-inclusive sketch pad, note pad and diary. When I got to our destination, I found a rich trove of photo-graphic opportunities.

Now, I could tell you a lot of facts about San Miguel, but they are available in other books and on the web. I thought I would share a few of my favorite photos and observations with you instead. After all, a photo is worth a 1,000 words or is it 10,000?

We recruited a local guide because we wanted to get off the beaten path, get tips on where to eat and what to see... to really enjoy our trip to the fullest. Bernardo was a fantastic help showing us around and getting us into some of the main attractions. He is an artist at heart who recently started creating papier mâché figures at La Aurora, in the studio of an artist friend.

Because he is fluent in several languages, Bernardo gained a reputation assisting expats assimilate into the Mexican culture of San Miguel de Allende. He turned out to be a valuable asset.

This is the third book in the series "*Where Is My Mind*." It starts differently, but it's purpose is the same as that of the two previous books - to tell a story, to entertain and to enlighten. Although it is more serious, with less of my off-the-wall humor, it starts with a list of very funny professional endorsements. (They are one page back. Take a look in case you missed them!)

So, after months of research and planning, we were finally in San Miguel, or SMA as the locals call it, and we were very glad we went!

This book started as **DOORS & MORE,,,**
but grew into this bigger project as
we walked around and experienced,,,
The Magic of San Miguel de Allende, Mexico.

This is just the beginning,,,

San Miguel de Allende:

When friends start talking about their most recent trip to Mexico, popular destinations like Cabo San Lucas, Mexico City, Guadalajara, Cancun, Puerto Vallarta, Cozumel and Tulum come to mind as Mexico's most popular destinations.

One evening, while having dinner together, friends who travel extensively excitedly told us about a trip they had just taken to San Miguel de Allende, Mexico. They raved about the culture, the architecture, the arts, the joyous atmosphere and the food.

My wife surprised me when she said that this city has been on her bucket list for many years too. I was surprised because it was the first time I heard about this. Why, I didn't even know where San Miguel was!

A few days later, while talking with my sister who lives in New York City, about the dinner we had with our friends, I was surprised again when she said that San Miguel was on her bucket list too.

This inspired me to find out more about San Miguel. Like my wife, I got excited about this destination and we scheduled a trip to go there. The four of us, my wife, my sister and her husband, were in for a fantastic vacation in central Mexico, in a city at about 6000 ft elevation in the Guanajuato Mountain Range and known as an artists colony with historic buildings dating back to the 15th century and a native culture that goes back even earlier.

The city was named after two people, a friar named Juan de San Miguel and Ignacio Allende, a martyr of the Mexican Independence revolution, who was born in a house on the city's central plaza.

Curiosity has taken us to many new and exciting places and San Miguel was to be our next destination.

It turned out to be lively and lovely. Trust me, if this town is not yet included in most Top Ten Destinations in Mexico, it will soon will be.

As the book was taking shape, a friend suggested that the title should be "Doors, Dolls & the Day-of-the-Dead,,, San Miguel on My Mind." Should have used this?

It is more descriptive, but doesn't tell the whole story.

The big picture: **DOORS & MORE,,,**

What is it about doors that fascinates many of us? The art and architecture of doors can be bold, colorful, modern, polished and antique. Some doors recall the grandeur of their past while others desperately need renovation.

Most doors beg to be opened. Some should remain closed. A door is the barrier between the known and the unknown.

My fascination with doors began many years ago with the popularity of posters like Doors of New Orleans, Doors of Cranbrook and Doors of Ireland, to name just a few.

Since door posters always intrigued me, I was finally inspired to create my own two posters: Doors of Tuscany and Doors of Italy. They were fun to design and both turned out great!

I had planned to do the same for the doors of San Miguel, but this story turned out to be different. It isn't just about doors, it's also about the friendly people and the rich culture we discovered during our two week stay in San Miguel.

And beware, because I threw in some of my wacky humor along the way,,, I hope you smile on this journey with me into a joyous land of vibrant color and exuberant customs.

I discovered the typical architecture here consists of thick stucco (now concrete) walls with small or no windows to the street and traditional carved wooden doors.

Stucco walls are painted, brick and stone walls retained their natural color. This type of construction is encouraged to this day to limit the heat of the intense sun and to keep homes cooler.

Most homes have interior courtyards where residents can enjoy a cooler, shady environment, while many exterior walls are rich with overhanging vines and flowers and roof tops are decorated with potted plants .

This is one of the many mysterious narrow alleys we discovered in San Miguel. Follow one to the end and what will you find? This city is full of surprises!

Our journey begins in the Historic Centro District,,,

The main church is the Parroquia de San Miguel Arcangel,,,

,,,a spectacular 17th-century neo-Gothic church in a Baroque city. The colors of the church change as the sun moves across the sky. This is probably the most striking and photographed site in San Miguel.

The interior is as
spectacular as the
exterior,,,
We were so impressed,
we returned many
times during our stay.

A nighttime view of the Centro district and the **Parroquia** as seen from a rooftop restaurant.

This 15th century Neo-Gothic Catholic Church overlooks El Jardin, the park in the heart of San Miguel. It's tall spires are often used as a visual reference point while wandering through the streets both day and night.

Templo de San Rafael
and
Templo de San Francisco

San Miguel has a
LOT of churches!

Meanwhile, back oh the street,,, No hablas Español,,, No problemo!

Getting around is easy. Because of the large American and Canadian expat community, English is understood and often spoken. You will find art is on display everywhere,,,

We walked or drove past this imposing, seemingly deserted building every day on our way to the Centro. Hard as we tried to find out what it was used for, we never did.

It remains an enigma. What added to the mystery was the statue. It was set off to the right, against the red wall, just out of sight on this page.

What was the purpose of the building? ? What did the sculpture mean? Who owned this place?

No one could tell us.

As we explored, we found it paid to keep our eyes open, and our cameras fully charged!!!

Where is My Mind??? Reading several books and listening to Bernardo filled me with local knowledge.

I had a desire to become a **_RHODES SCHOLAR_**,,, you know, a wise guy with an education from that famous place in England,,,

,,,but I was slowed down by a speed bump and the closest I could get to my goal was to gain a few **street smarts** *and to* be awarded the degree of

SCHOLAR
of the
ROADS,,,

Which meant that I could now read a map and give directions to local attractions such as the local Starbucks, but only in English.

Bernardo was not in fear of me taking over his role as a guide and found my attempts funny.

Giants Walk Among Us,,,
The Traditional Mojiganga Parade

One of the more intriguing sights that greeted us were dozens of huge dolls, usually female. They were both intimidating and charming, ten feet tall or so, standing guard in doorways, hanging around hotel lobbies and mixing with pedestrians on the street like royalty among the commoners.

One day, as I walked down a quiet residential street, vibrantly colored buildings glowing in the afternoon sun, Parque Benito Juarez came into view. Lush foliage and tree-shaded paths stretched in every direction. Ahead of me was a large gazebo which overflowed with elegantly dressed people dancing to the lively strains of Mariachi music.

This looked interesting, and although Bernardo was not with us, we went over to take a look.

Suddenly, two gigantic human forms were towering above me. I was caught up in the lively rhythms of the Mariachi band and swept through the park with the happy whirlwind of wedding-goers from Atlanta, Georgia. Punctuated by peals of laughter and well lubricated with tequila, it was a Mexican folk-fairytale come true!

Who were these two towering strangers, dancing and whirling around me, who then suddenly passed by me with a swish of taffeta and the rustle of beads...

They were Mojigangas, or Gigantes, as they are sometimes called, puppets which originated in Spain and were brought to Mexico in the 1600's. They were once created to make fun of public figures and used to lighten the mood during somber religious pilgrimages. The word "Mojiganga" means "burlesque" so these paper giants are meant to exaggerate and make fun of our human foibles and weaknesses.

The head and upper body of the Mojigangas are made of papier-mâché, mounted on a frame 8 to18 feet tall and carried by a puppeteer whose only connections with the outside world are his feet and a peephole through which he navigates the parade route.

If you fall in love with the Mojigangas, you can rent or buy one to parade in the streets of San Miguel or to ship home and store in a closet until the right opportunity presents itself for a Gringo Mojiganga parade!

San Miguel has become a mecca for destination weddings with over 700 celebrated annually. Wedding parades called Callejoneadas are a tradition here.

They feature Mojigangas leading the way, followed by marching bands, joyful wedding participants and a burro who carries the tequila to make sure the wedding party stays well hydrated.

When not on parade, our friends stand guard and serve as inspiration for tourist fun and frivolity,,,

Not all gals are made of sugar, spice and everything nice.

I like those made of sarcasm, wine and everything fine,,,

Wedding parades, called **Callejoneadas**, complete with a mariachi band are a tradition here,,,

Lets put this all together:

A San Miguel wedding,

Giant **Mojigangas** leading a parade, called a **Callejoneada**,

a **Mariachi** marching band,

and an adorable **Burro** supplying the **tequila**,

How can this combination miss???

After lunch we got back to exploring the streets of the Centro district and taking photos of this charming town,,,

Inviting streets, picturesque buildings and a vibrant artist community went hand-in-hand with our leisurely stroll,,,

A part of the magic we experienced was the color. Rich and vibrant colors can be found throughout this city. Bright sun and shadows add up to great photographic opportunities. In this photo the door makes an aristocratic focal point.

The next day, as we continued our explorations, we began to notice many statues and skulls in shops and museums. At first, I thought these were kind of morbid.

So I had to ask Bernardo, "WHY?" and he explained the tradition to me.

These fanciful **skeletons** and **skulls** are meant to celebrate **the Day of the Dead** and are a playful symbol of life after death.

At times they represent people who have died while enjoying their favorite activities.
This is a celebration of life, not sadness and death. There are parties with drinks and food, lots of food! Skulls made out of sugar are a popular part of these celebrations.

Día de los Muertos
Day of the Dead celebrations

The skull is used not as a ghoulish symbol but rather as a droll reminder of the cyclicality of life, which is why they are brightly decorated.

The Aztec and Maya people also held celebrations to commemorate their deceased loved ones, a practice that pre-dates the landing of the Spanish Conquistadors by 3,000 years .

Calaveritas de azucar, or sugar skulls, along with toys, are left on the altars for children who have passed away.

The belief of ancient Mesoamericans was that death is part of the journey of life. Death does not end life, but it was believed that new life comes from death. This cycle is often associated with the cyclical nature of agriculture, when crops grow from the ground where the last crops lie buried.

We were in San Miguel in the early spring, but we were told Monarch butterflies play a role in *Día de los Muertos* because they are believed to hold the spirits of the departed.

This belief stems from the fact that the first monarchs arrive in Mexico for the winter each fall on Nov.1, which coincides with *Día de los Muertos*.

Float like a butterfly, sting like a bee!

What are the chances of me ever growing up?

One evening we stopped for dinner and some adult refreshments at an upscale disco bar and night club, located in the Centro District.

The entrance was intriguing but not off-putting. Instead, it promised a new adventure in dining, and we weren't disappointed.

The food and atmosphere were truly outstanding!

We finished the day on a cobble-stone street, with a speed bump.

In fact, speed bumps are required and found on almost every street, since there are NO stop signs or traffic lights at any of the intersections.

The drivers are all very courteous and respectful of both pedestrians and other vehicular traffic.

In a city of great doors, you will occasionally see one that shows great promise, but needs a carpenter and a paint brush to restore it's original grandeur!

This door grabbed my attention!

Why?

It is the entrance to a Bakery!

My grandfather was a baker and I spent my formative years in an apartment above the working kitchen. I grew up with the aroma of fresh bread coming out of the oven every morning.

Please notice,,, **No signs**, but the smells of fresh bread drifted out onto the street and I could not resist...

What's Behind The Front Door?

As we continued exploring San Miguel, we had an opportunity to visit a typical interior courtyard. Outdoor living rooms are a tradition dating back to Roman times.

As I described earlier, this space provides the residents with ample shade and serves as their private oasis away from the heat, noise and traffic of El Centro.

Here's a contemporary door that blends in very well with other more ornate traditional doors on the street.

Bright sunlight creates vivid shadows, adding drama to the rich colors of this home, while flower pots decorate the roof-top, a frequent sight in the Centro.

The doors of San Miguel provide a
focal point and add interest to an
otherwise featureless stucco wall.

Cañada de la Virgen

One day, Bernardo made arrangements for us to take a trip to an archaeological site dating back to the Otomi indigenous people of the central Mexican Plateau. This historical site dates back to about 530 AD.

Located in Guanajuato Province, this site is home to one of the 6 original civilizations of the planet and one of the two cultural columns of contemporary Mexico. ***

Cañada de la Virgen
Zona Arqueológica

***When the first humans started to give up the hunter-gather lifestyle and started to settle down in one place, six distinct cradles of civilization came into being and can be clearly identified. They are Mesopotamia (Iraq and Iran), Egypt, the Indus Valley (Pakistan and Afghanistan), Mexico and Peru, and China. The first five began around 3000 BCE, while the Chinese civilization started around 2100 BCE. Each of these civilizations developed near a river.

The Otomi worshiped the moon, the sun and Venus as well as various other gods, each of whom symbolized a natural force which was synchronized with the growing seasons of their food crops.

The site faces the celestial north, where the stars spin around in a circle during the year. The moon moves up and down the stairs during it's phases, setting and rising in the notch at the top of the pyramid at solstice.

The site is located on private land. The first excavation began in1995, while the official excavation began in 2002. Our tour guide was one of the original archeologists involved in the excavation.

The Otomi people have lived in the area for thousands of years and about 42,000 of them still do, speaking their own language and retaining some religious practices from the old days. Evidence shows that **Cañada De La Virgen** was constructed around 540 CE and abandoned around 1040 CE.

The Otomi were avid sky watchers and passed information down from generation to generation about solstice periods. They integrated astronomical data and agricultural cycles with religious beliefs.

This ceremonial center is one of the keys to understanding one of the original cultures of Mexico, and its complex pre-Hispanic indigenous civilization.

This may be more information than you were expecting from this book, but if you are hungry for more, there's lots more available on the internet. It is a long, complex and fascinating history!

No vacation or holiday is complete without a shopping spree.

Now, these folks, perhaps wealthy tourists, will *hopefully* buy some opal.

Then, with the profit, the Opal Mine's door will *hopefully* get some much-needed TLC!

A peek through an iron gate, up a few stairs to an outdoor courtyard and the imposing main entrance of St. Paul's Anglican Episcopal Church comes in to view. They have a truly lovely setting with a well-tended and beautifully landscaped garden.

Can your attention span take a few more doors???

Two doors, one demonstrating success and status, the other security,,,

A welcoming entry gate leading to a shady outdoor courtyard greets both pedestrians and guests arriving on 2-wheeled vehicles. When you live on such narrow streets, often parking on the sidewalk is your only option.

This minimalist door betrays the personality of it's owner... unpretentious, to the point and self confident

Here's a wall with a vibrant wash of color, wood doors set in a wrought iron frame and a gaggle of electric meters,,, This must be a Multi-Family Apartment or Condominium, probably with a large interior courtyard since there are no windows visible to the street.

GUÍA DE AVES
del Charco del Ingenio

San Miguel de Allende

Guanajuato

México

Bernardo took us to explore the **Charco del Ingenio**, a 170 acre nature preserve and botanical garden.

It is a magical place with numerous cactus species, birds and animals native to this dry land. Some are very rare, even in danger of extinction.

The name translates into English as "The Mill Puddle." It derives from a spring-fed pond in the canyon whose gushing water once powered San Miguel's La Aurora textile mill.

The canyon used to be an overgrazed community dump. Then a non-profit from SMA cleaned it up and on July 11th, 1991, during a total solar eclipse, reopened it to the public as a botanical garden and nature preserve. It offers sanctuary to endangered species. There are walking trails, guided tours and a welcome center with a gift store and a snack bar.

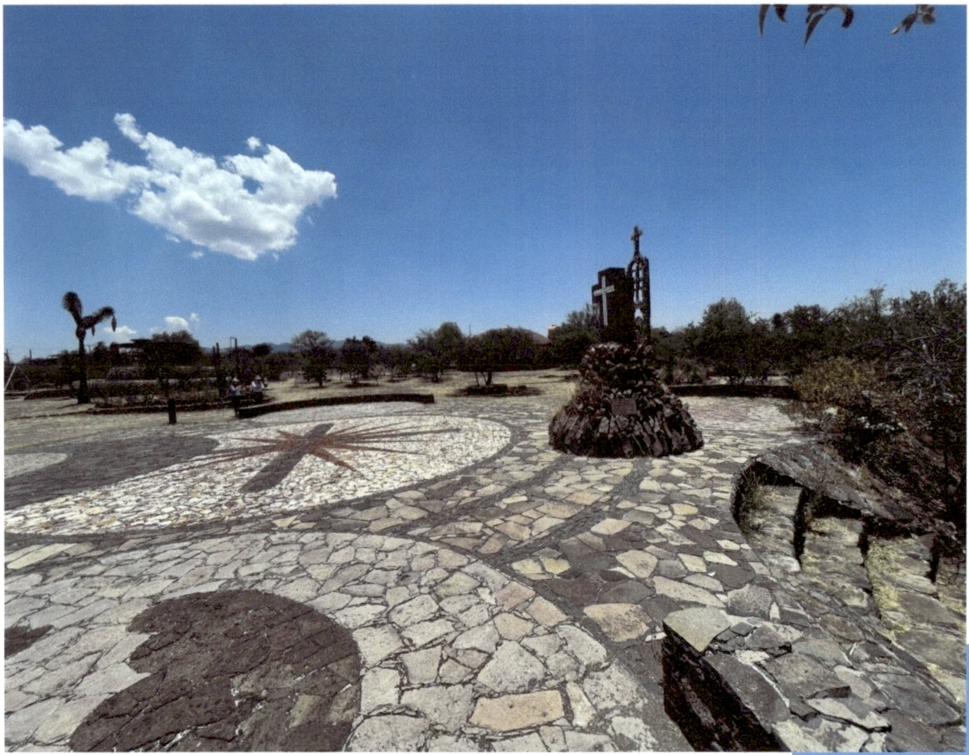
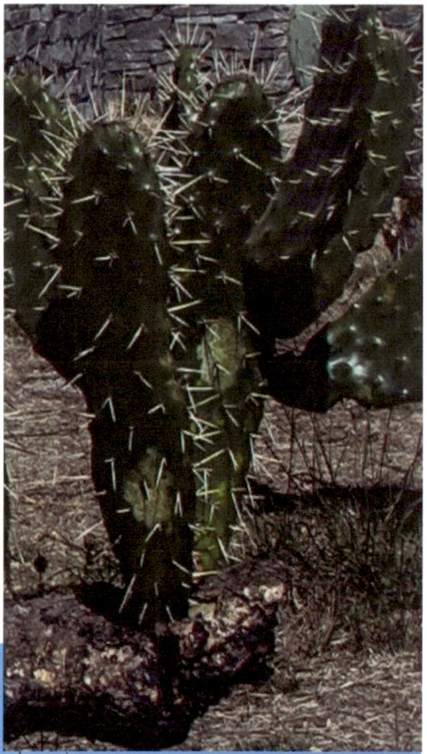
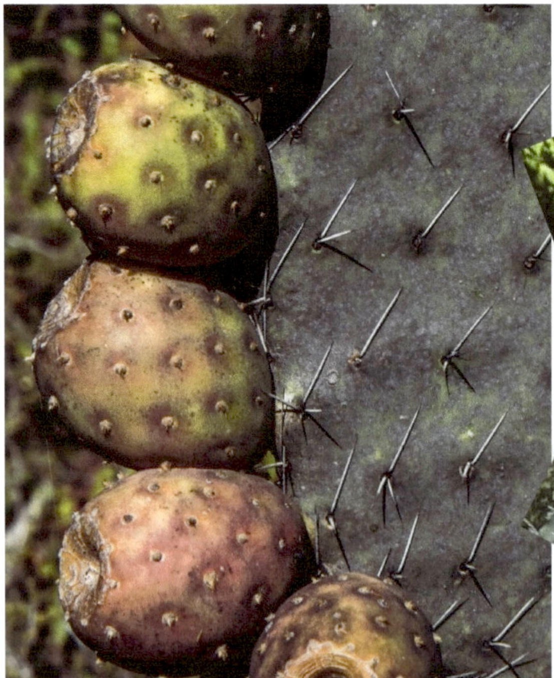
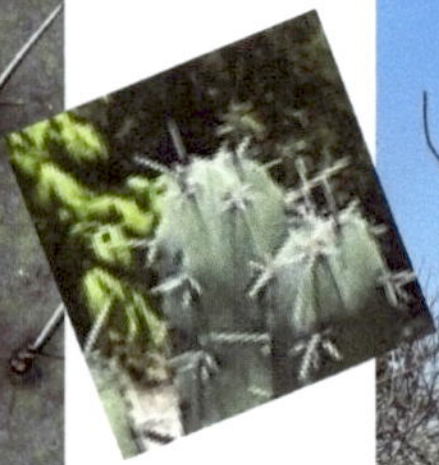
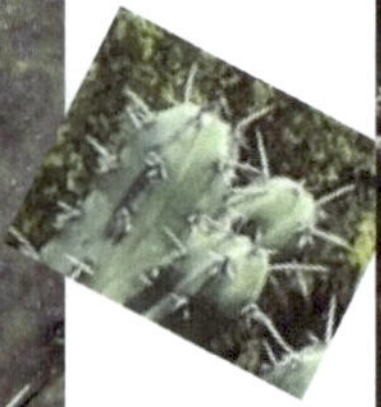
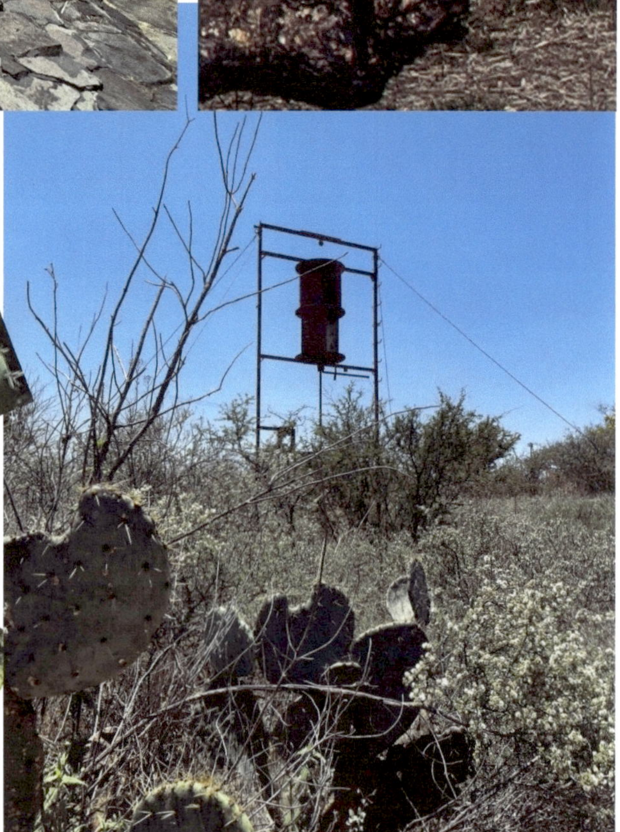

The House of Starlight, a short hike from the entrance to Charco del Ingenio, was designed by a German artist named Wilhelm Holderied. It is an enigmatic pyramid-like structure which you can climb. It reminded me of the Otomi ruins at Canada de la Virgen. Modern historic ruins! Cool!

The Welcome Center housing a gift shop (below) was architecturally interesting as well.

The El Charco spring was dammed in the 1920's, creating a picturesque lake and reservoir. It is interesting to note that archeological evidence of an aqueduct built by the Conquistadors to bring water to San Miguel from the El Charco remains to this day, a relic much like Otomi ruins. The textile mill in San Miguel had been powered by the spring since the 16th century until it was converted into Fabrica la Aurora, today a major art and design center with galleries and artists' workshops.

When we visited the preserve, it's once huge lake was bone dry. We were told that it is now seasonal and can no longer be depended on as a reservoir. It's bottom was exposed, dry, cracked into geometric shapes, completely devoid of life. How sad,,,

Fabrica La Aurora,,,

We took the better part of a day to explore La Aurora, the massive textile mill complex which is now home to art galleries, artisan shops, outdoor exhibits and working studios.

We enjoyed the opportunity to meet the artists in person, in their own studios, while they were in the process of working at creating their art.

We also included a break for lunch. The options are many,,, you can enjoy everything from a glass of wine and fine tapas to a great burger!

**Whoa,
Big Fella,,,**
Aurora was great fun! While no one was looking, I got my trusty lasso out and tamed this rearing stallion!

Hey,,,
Marshal Dillon,,,
I could have been a cowboy!!!

I must admit, I really get into the spirit of a work of art when it moves me… when I experience the raw power of creative thought, Walter-Mitty style. Fortunately, I didn't get myself into trouble ,,,this time...

Back out on the
street,
I saw vibrant colors
in bright sunshine,,,

This was art too!
Struck by inspiration,
I had to capture
this unforgettable
image!

"I hear you knock-
ing, but you can't
come in,,,"

,,,an audacious
response, they must
have thought I was
a bill collector or
the meter reader,,,

Out came my camera once more. This was truly an unforgettable door. Rumor is that it is the former home of the,,,

San Miguel Uranium & Plutonium Company!

I wonder if it glows in the dark?

If you're looking for a project,,, here is one that can be had at a BARGAIN!!!

I really liked
the effect
of pots
decorating
rooftops,,,
something I
have seen
nowhere else.
And the color
in the
sunbeams,,,

Every door has its own soul, and its own unique interior,, It is up to you to open it,,,

And now on to dinner, to the historic El Manantial which has been serving great food for100+ years!!!
9:00PM and there is still a waiting line!!!

Color is used to enhance our environments. Color can evoke many moods in the viewer. Red is considered to be a color of intense emotions. It can symbolize strength, confidence, and power. It is also associated with love.

Some people believe that gates are as important as doors. In some cases, that may be true, however, another observation could be that it probably creates a false sense of security. Sort of like the analogy of the man that secures his pants with both a belt and suspenders.

So many people are
judgmental, I can tell
just by looking at them,,,

Quite a color scheme!
Violet, lavender, pumpkin orange and cherry red,,,
Does this door belong to a mild
eccentric, perhaps a mildly
eccentric expat?

The color purple is associated
with royalty and luxury.

13A - One of my favorite
numbers, and some of my
favorite colors,,,

My daughter was born on a
Friday the 13th,,,

A great place for the '**motorcycle gang**' to hang out,,,

The '**Caballeros**' are probably *not* going for a haircut or a tire iron!!!

This photo was taken in a commercial district. Three shops in a row: a barbershop, a blacksmith making balconies, doors & railings and a restaurant/pizzeria,,,

Meet "Mr. Invincible," as a large ego meets "Street Art"

Inspired by the books I have been reading, I decided that I would have a sporting session with this El Toro,,, He seemed very agreeable. In fact, he challenged me to assume 'the position' and hold out my red cape!

**And later that day,
at the entrance to LIVE AQUA Urban Spa,,,**

I was greeted by an enormous sculpture titled *CABEZA VAINILLA*. A famous Mexican sculptor, Javier Marin, created this dramatic piece out of polyester resin and iron. It is one of a set of three giant heads currently on display throughout Mexico. They make a dramatic impression wherever they are exhibited.

As my Mom often said to me, "You can pick your friends, but you can't pick your nose,,, in public"

This distinguished pair of doors, one a front entry for people, the other for automobiles, hark back to an era of elegance. Our cab driver commented **"Doors like this start to grow on you."** True. Especially when the entire façade is covered with ivy!

I read that people all over the world are attracted to DOORS,,, especially *locksmiths*!

Just because a door appears closed, it does not mean that it is locked - nor that it will not open with the right heart, call or touch.
You are the key that opens it.

A doctor friend told me that looking at this diverse display of DOOR KNOCKERS would be extremely stressful for a person with a case of Knock-ta-phobia,,, the fear of backing into a door knocker while naked.

He went on to explain that this is different from Nyctophobia, which is a fear of darkness. Good to know!

I bet it takes a firm hand to open *this* door! Kind of creepy, don't you think?

Many other things surprised me about San Miguel,,, including electric meters secured by ornate grilles and padlocks.

Why lock up your electric meter if it won't stop a determined thief?

Look at the cut wires on the meter to the left,,, a thief could attach his wire to it, run it along the sidewalk to his house and steal your power! This would be silly in the US, but electric wiring is such a free-form art in San Miguel, no one would notice!

This is what I mean,,,

Here I am, in magical San Miguel de Allende, sinking into the culture, eating delicious local food, ogling the sights like any good tourist, but I also find myself photographing creative electrical installations, of which there are plenty!

I must confess,,.
I am an electrical engineer.

And here's another one!

"Lord, please give me the patience and help me bite my tongue,,,"

Even though
there are
a lot of
churches in
San Miguel, I'm
afraid this door
needs more
than prayer!!!

Mabely,,,
is a bar,,, and a very
nice one at that. We
had a good time there,,,

Some of the photos are
easily recognizable,
others not so much.

Several of my friends
suggested that I include
the address of each
door in this book.

I thought about it for
some time and came to
the conclusion that
some people may feel
their privacy was com-
promised, so I decided
against it.

All that matters is that
they are all from San
Miguel, photographed in
the spring of 2022, and
will remain an
anonymous testament
to what this fair city
looked like at the time.

Sunny on the outside,,, but could there be "Shady" characters behind these doors?

I'm not a shady character, but I'd definitely enjoy living in this elegant home. Who wouldn't?

No Bull! This could be the SMA Adult Bookstore & Senior Day Care Center,,,

Do you think a few shots of Tequila could straighten this photo out?

Taking a 'Time Out,' Bernardo insisted that we enjoy the many culinary delights of his city,,,

Virtually all the doors are wood or metal. We did not see any architectural glass doors. Most wood doors are very intricately carved or constructed with unique designs. A few doors have been painted. We saw many that need to be painted again.

Here's a good example of some very intricate carving on a door.

Going to ....

Once regal but now in bad need of total renovation.

.... Extremes

Beautifully main-
tained and lovingly
decorated.

This was the only example of a side entry that I saw in all of San Miguel.

One of the many doorways that was OPEN for Business,,,

A catchy slogan to promote this business might read:
"No Thrill, just Drill, Fill, & Bill, as easy as ..."
I don't know. Pain doesn't rhyme.

Here I was, on a mission looking for interesting doors to photograph. It was getting late in the day,,,

Just as I tried to focus on this door, a woman walking by saw me. She appeared to be interested in my work.

As she came closer, my heart beat quickened. Will she ask about my photography? Has she *seen* my work?

But instead she said "Your fly is open, sir."

Number 1: I was embarrassed.

Number 2: Where did she get such good eyesight?

Number 3: Why did this middle-aged woman call me sir? I'm not THAT old!

A very creative touch, a colorful
sculpted figure sitting on a chair
on a 2nd story balcony,,,

Notice the addresses,,,

Now, here is a unique door bell.
Is this guy spitting at me???
Should I press his nose to get him to stop?

Another
entrance that
grows on you,

Certainly elegant
and welcoming,,,

"I bought that hat to protect his head from the sun.

Now look at him over there,,,

His behavior is out-rageous!

I'll pretend I'm not looking…"

"Look at her…
She's pretending she doesn't
see me.

First of all, modesty is a virtue
I hold very dear.

Second, who says I can't ride
a turtle when I want to?

It's never too late for a
happy childhood."

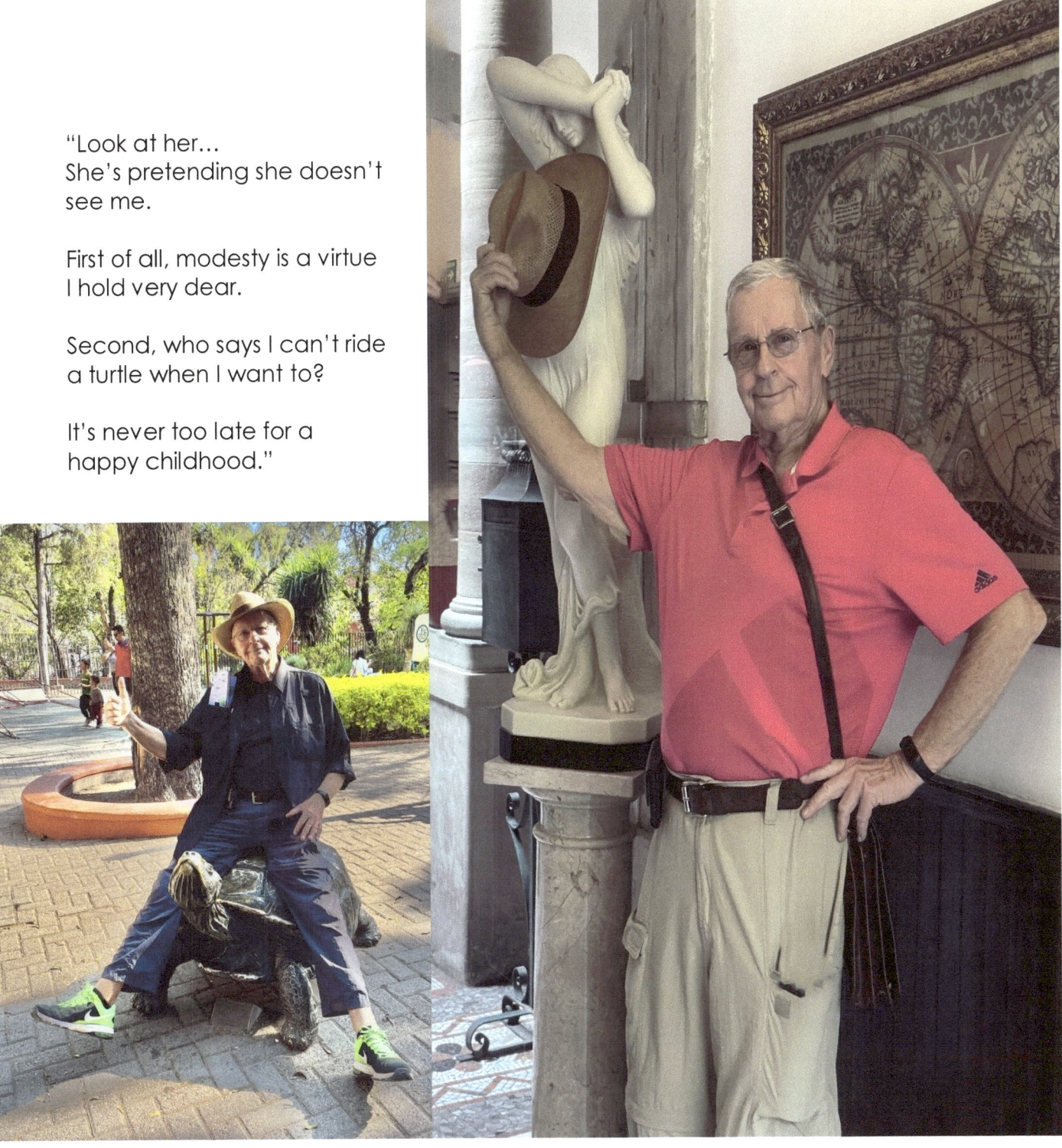

The color orange invokes a sense of success and sociability. It also makes me think of orange juice.

We did not see many street vendors. Most vendors in SMA work out of food carts.

But we did see this one enterprising young man. What do you think he was selling?

I'll give you one guess and a hint,,, It wasn't hats.

Some designers believe the color blue suggests creativity and happiness.

It must have been a design trend in *South Living* to put BLUE DOORS and a TALL CACTUS together,,,

This trend was short lived,,,

Before you know it, a clever neighbor painted his door blue and put in TWO cactus next to it, and voila! A new trend was born.

And, finally, magical San Miguel de Allende
left me with a profound mystery
which I leave for you to solve,,,

Why is this bush here?

Is it part of their security system?
How long have the owners been gone?
Is there a back door?

Magical mysteries notwithstanding,
many, many thanks, Bernardo.
You were a great host and guide.
You became our friend.
We hope to see you soon on our next trip to
San Miguel de Allende.

www.ingramcontent.com/pod-product-compliance
Lightning Source LLC
Chambersburg PA
CBHW041616120626
46551CB00003B/466